LIFE LESSONS FROM ELVIS

LIFE LESSONS FROM

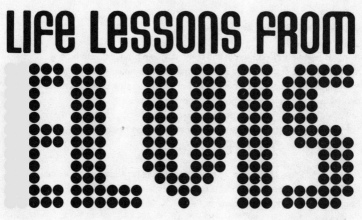

ELVIS

a parody

· ·

ANTHONY RUBINO JR.

RUTLEDGE HILL PRESS®

Nashville, Tennessee

A Division of Thomas Nelson Publishers
www.thomasnelson.com

Published by Rutledge Hill Press, a Division of Thomas Nelson, Inc., P.O. Box 141000, Nashville, Tennessee 37214.

Rutledge Hill Press books may be purchased in bulk for educational, business, fund-raising, or sales promotional use. For information, please e-mail SpecialMarkets@ThomasNelson.com.

The photo on page 159 is adapted from a photo in the National Archives.

Library of Congress Cataloging-in-Publication Data

Rubino, Anthony, 1966–
  Life lessons from Elvis : a parody / Anthony Rubino Jr.
    p. cm.
ISBN 1-4016-0248-7
1. Presley, Elvis, 1935–1977—Humor. I. Title.
PN6231.P695R93 2006
818'.602—dc22   2006000662

Printed in China
06 07 08 09 10 — 5 4 3 2 1

TO THOSE FRIENDS OF MINE WHO AIN'T
NEVER CAUGHT A RABBIT

SPECIAL THANKS

Extra special thanks to Elvis for existing and for being everything he is to so many people. A book like this would not be possible if he wasn't so unassailably cool.

Special thanks to all those people who followed Elvis around and said things like: Gold toilet seats are not just attractive, but practical; If you're gonna buy one Cadillac, you might as well buy three; No, E, that jumpsuit does not make you look fat.

Thanks to my family and friends for their love and support.

Thanks to my agent, Jim McCarthy, who thought this was a funny idea, and sold it.

And thanks to Bryan Curtis at Rutledge Hill Press for buying it.

INTRODUCTION

So I'm having lunch with Elvis the other day . . . and the King of Rock 'n' Roll turned to me, looked me right in the eye, and said, "Hey, uh . . . Tony, man, uh . . . you gonna finish those french fries?"

"Well, Elvis," I said, "I've only had one, but if you really want them then—"

"Thank you. Thankyavrrymuch," he said and took the remainder of my fries. "You know, man, there ain't nothin' more satisfyin' than an extra helpin' of french fries with a couple-a large chicken-fried steaks." He leaned back and swallowed hard. "Except for maybe, washin' down six or seven fried peanut butter and banana sandwiches with a couple gallons-a milk," he finished with a wink.

"Wow," I thought, while E chewed noisily, "that's deep." And just then it hit me like a karate chop from the King himself!

"Elvis," I said, "with all the experience and wisdom you have, you ought to write a book."

Without looking up, he shook his head and said, "Naw, naw, man. I'm way too busy to be writin' any books right now, T. You know, I promised Jim Morrison I'd help him with his new disguise. Then I'm backpackin' through Europe with Jimmy Hoffa. After that

I'm due to get spotted at a convenience store out in Tulsa. Then I got that thing with—"

I held up my hand and interrupted. "You're right. You're right. You're way too busy. It is a shame, though," I said with a sigh. "People could benefit a great deal from your wisdom, King."

He stopped chewing for a moment. "Well, why don't you just go ahead an' write it for me, man?" he said. Then he took a long pull from a two-liter bottle of Coke.

"Me?" I replied, surprised. "Why, I couldn't—"

"Sure," belched Elvis. "I mean, you know me better'n just 'bout anybody, except for my dearly departed mother, rest her soul—"

"Rest her soul," I said simultaneously.

"And you've already written a couple-a those type-a books, man. Why, you'd be perfect for it!"

"You know what, E?" I said. "You're right! I can write that book for you. Furthermore, I would be honored to write it on your behalf." I placed my hands on the table, slowly began to rise, and said, "I will bestow upon the world . . . " I paused, noticing all eyes in the diner upon me as I leaned back down and whispered, "What should we call it, E?"

And through a full mouth he said, "I don't know . . . uh . . . Life Lessons from Me, I reckon."

I bolted upright and said triumphantly, *"Life Lessons from Elvis!"* I stood there, my bosom heaving, my tear-streaked face thrust skyward, as Elvis absently sopped up some grease with what was left of a jelly doughnut. And that's how the King of Rock 'n' Roll and I conceived of this monumental tome.

So now you hold in your hands the fruits of our labor—a life lesson book wherein advice about the strange and bizarre mingles effortlessly with words of wisdom on the mundane and practical—from velvet to Velveeta!

So stretch out on the couch in your jungle room, move over that big ceramic monkey on the coffee table, put your feet up, and take hold of a big hunka-hunka burnin' life as seen through the eyes of the original American idol.

But beware! This advice is not just deep—it's deep-fried.

—ANTHONY RUBINO JR.

LIFE LESSONS FROM ELVIS

Never wear a belt buckle that's bigger than your head.

Ya gotta count yer blessings. For example, I'm thankful people call me "Elvis the Pelvis." My name coulda been Rick, man.

No use cryin' over spilt milk. Unless you just ate four peanut butter sandwiches and a whole fried chicken. Then I can't think of a better reason to cry.

If you wind up in jail as prisoner number 33, and number 47 tells you that you're the cutest jailbird he ever did see, you're in big trouble there, man.

If you're looking for a commemorative quilt or some sort of hokey wood-carving souvenir, don't expect to find it at Graceland. That's *so* Dollywood.

Gyrate responsibly.

The best advice I ever got was when I was nineteen and my boss at Precision Tools in Memphis told me to "shake a leg." Now, it never did me no good as a delivery truck driver, but it worked out just fine for my other career.

Wear your life like a loose set of clothes. Wear your clothes like a sausage casing.

It's a small world. Just look at that "six degrees of Kevin Bacon" thing. Priscilla is Lisa Marie's mom. She was in *Naked Gun* with Leslie Nielsen. Leslie Nielsen was in the movie *Airplane*. I had an airplane named *Lisa Marie*. And I *love* bacon. See what I mean? Small world . . .

People are people. Shoot! When you get right down to it, I'm just like you—really. I put on my jumpsuit one leg at a time and then one arm at a time, just like everybody else.

Durable. Stain resistant and wrinkle free. I tell ya what, man, I don't care if it does burst into flames every now and again. That's a small price to pay for the miracle that is polyester.

There's a fine line between garbage and artifact.

Surround yourself with a diverse staff. I had a person who'd take my car to be washed . . . a person who'd take messages for me . . . a person who'd take dictation for me . . . and a person who'd take a bullet for me.

Once and for all, don't believe it when people say they saw me out at some bowling alley. I mean that's just ridiculous, man! I don't bowl.

When you're courting a young lady, it's important to get on her parents' good side. So be respectful. Say "Yes sir" and "Yes ma'am." Show 'em that you're mature and sincere. Oh, it also helps to give them a check for $10,000 to remodel their home.

Don't be pretentious. There's no need to put your name up in flashing 500-watt bulbs when 400 watts'll do just fine.

Keep an eye on your toddler. Especially if your property has a large, unruly wild area where a child might get lost. Lisa Marie gave us a scare one time when she went missing. We finally found her in Priscilla's hair, but it was touch and go for a while.

It's not how much you know . . . it's how much
leather you wear.

Ya ever been at a fast-food restaurant and thought you spotted me gettin' some french fries or somethin'? No? Well you ain't goin' to the right fast-food restaurants, man.

You can tell a lot about a person by where they were born. Being from Mississippi I was greatly influenced by gospel music. Priscilla, on the other hand, was born in Brooklyn near the water, which I guess explains why she was so influenced by Aqua Net.

Remember: only one portrait of yourself per room or people'll think you're conceited.

If you want somethin' done right, you gotta do it yourself. So be sure you're the one who hires the right person to do it for you.

A good way to make some spare cash is to find a vegetable that looks just like me. Man, you'd be surprised how many people will pay good money to see a turnip that's shaped like my head.

If you're gonna do an Elvis impersonation, don't do that thing where you turn your back to the audience, comb your hair, and flip up yer collar. I never did that, man, I always showed up that way.

You can take the boy out of Tupelo, but you can't take Tupelo out of the boy.

Don't be afraid to ask the tough questions. Things like "What is our purpose in this vast universe? Why must so many people in this world suffer so very much? What will become of us after we die?" And "Am I wearing shoes, cuz I haven't been able to see my feet in two years?"

Be careful when someone gives you advice. My momma once told me to be myself and not to act like somebody I'm not. Well, she meant in *life,* but I went ahead and did it in all thirty of my films.

Women love to feel special. So never go on a
date with more than two at a time.

Material things can't make you happy. But then again, they don't make you sad, neither.

Don't fear the sneer.

Money can't buy love, but it sure does buy a lotta fried chicken!

In a pinch, a 22-caliber pistol makes an
excellent TV remote control. But you can
only use it once.

Feelin' a little bit insecure? Surround yourself with people who call you by your first initial, laugh at all your jokes, and agree with everything you say.

It's pivot, thrust, point, kick, turn, gyrate, karate chop. *Not* thrust, point, kick, turn, gyrate, karate chop, pivot! If you're gonna impersonate me, do it right, man!

If I am getting a Slurpee at a 7-Eleven in Tuscaloosa, but nobody spots me, am I there?

If you love something, set it free. If it comes back, it was always yours. If it doesn't come back or if its father won't let it, lock it up in yer mansion until it's of consenting legal age.

Don't be friends with somebody who's never caught a rabbit.

Be responsible with your gold lamé suits. I once walked out of a diner wearin' one on a sunny day. I nearly blinded a man, man.

Teach your daughters to stay away from weirdo, man-child, plastic-surgery-happy freaks.

You can't appreciate getting filthy rich unless you grow up dirt poor.

Really man, it's *never* too early to start teachin'
your daughters to stay away from weirdo, man-
child, plastic-surgery-happy freaks. Now, I
know I said that twice, but I can't emphasize
this one enough.

Don't be cruel . . . and tell a fella his shoe's untied when you know darn well he can't see his feet!

Just once I'd like to see one-a these impersonators stop for a minute, turn around, and say: "I'd like to give you my impression of Elvis. My impression of Elvis is that he seems like a nice fella." Is that too much to ask, man?

The right cape can be very slimming.

If you're itchin' like a man on a fuzzy tree, and your friends say you're actin' wild as a bug, you might very well be in love. Either that, or you took one too many of those green pills.

Never underestimate the power of your
upper lip.

After you've gained a few pounds, use caution when bending over in your sequined leather jumpsuit. If it's too snug, one of those sequins is liable to shoot right across the room and put somebody's eye out.

Where there's a will, there's plenty of residuals for everybody.

Speak clearly! I once had this karate teacher tell me I needed to meditate. Well, is it me, or does "meditate" sound a lot like "medicate"?

Here's a fun thing to do when you're bored:

Close your eyes. Then spin around three times.
Now reach out and take hold-a the first thing
that you touch. Open your eyes. OK, now get it
gold plated! If it's already gold plated, try again!

Punctuate with your body, man. For example, I'd say, "Hey, Red, go on and get me another couple gallons-a ice cream!" Then I'd thrust my right hip out, casually point with my left hand, tilt my head, wink, and finish by sayin', "Rocky Roooooooad."

Here's how to apply this to everyday life. Let's say you're in an office setting. Walk on up to your boss and say, "Hey boss, here are those photocopies you asked for—" Then bend your right knee slightly, lift your right heel up, and lock your left knee. Now quickly alternate that from left to right three or four times and finish with "—double sided."

If you look over your shoulder and all you can see is polyester and sequins, you're wearin' a high collar, man. But that's OK! That *is* OK! Just remember you got that blind spot; be aware of it and keep on rockin'!

Be careful what you say to your kids. I once told Lisa Marie that a skinny little child-like fella with a squeaky voice made a good companion. Shoot! I was talkin' 'bout our pet monkey, man!

People ask me, "E, why'd you wear that giant belt with a jumpsuit? Your pants were attached to your shirt—ain't that redundant?" Well, that's like askin' why I wore sunglasses when my eyes were closed most of the time anyway, cuz I was asleep! It's just one-a those things, man.

You get a way better deal if you buy horses in bulk.

When you ask for a pound-a bacon with your two cheese omelets, be specific! There's a big difference between a pound-a raw bacon and a pound-a cooked bacon. Make sure they weigh it after they cook it or you're liable to wind up with no more than half-a pound.

You know that saying, "Impersonation is the greatest form of flattery"? Yeah, I don't know about that one, man.

With greatness comes responsibility. And with responsibility comes a whole staff of people to do all the stuff you don't wanna do so you don't have to deal with all that responsibility.

Never wear metal-based fabric
in a thunderstorm.

Be tolerant of your neighbors. This one time at Graceland, one-a my bodyguards accidentally ran over my neighbor's cat. Well, she got all bent out-a shape. But come on, man! That sort-a thing is just gonna happen from time to time when you install a go-cart track on your property for a bunch-a drunk grown men.

You never know where you're gonna find inspiration. In 1946 I bought my very first guitar from a Tupelo hardware store. Just like that, I went from fixin' to fix somethin', to fixin' to be famous.

Be patient! No matter how bad you're jonesin'
for that fried peanut butter and banana
sandwich right after yer cook pops it off the
skillet and out of the sizzling butter, let it cool
man, let it cool.

I've found that you only go around once . . .
unless you rent the whole amusement park.

When you write somebody a thank-you note, try real hard to make it as personal as possible. Use a U.S. postage stamp with your picture on it, for example. Oh . . . sorry . . . right . . . there might not be a U.S. postage stamp with your picture on it. Well, just go ahead and stick a stamp on there from another country with your picture on it. Oh . . . right . . . um . . . well, dot your *i*'s with smiley faces or somethin'. I don't know, man . . . do I have to tell you everything?

Gold lamé suits are not just snazzy, but functional. They drive the ladies wild, and on a hot day you can fry an egg on your lapel.

Watch where you point them hips. I once double-thrusted on stage in Tulsa and a woman's head exploded.

If sequined jumpsuits are wrong, then I don't wanna be right, baby!

It helps a person to reminisce. Every now and then, I'll take out an old photo of Priscilla and me cuttin' our wedding cake and I'll think to myself, "Now that was a right fine cake!"

They say that great men are only great because they stand on the shoulders of giants. Well, to that I say, "John Lennon, Mick Jagger, Michael Jackson, Elton John, Bono, and all you other fellas—wipe your feet, cuz you're gettin' my jumpsuit dirty!"

Always wear your lei on the *outside* of your gargantuan collar.

Pork chops, country ham, bacon, chicken-fried steak. Candied yams, corn on the cob, apple pie, ice cream, and cake. Yep, breakfast is the most important meal of the day!

It's gonna lose value as soon as you drive it off the lot. So you'd be better off buyin' your 747 slightly used.

If you ask Sam Phillips at Sun Records, he'll tell you he discovered me. But if you ask me, I discovered Sam Phillips and Sun Records. It's all a matter of perspective, man.

There's nothin' like the look in her eyes when you give your little girl her very first monogrammed golf cart.

Great men are defined by their homes. Thomas Jefferson's Monticello introduced classic Italian living spaces to the New World. Frank Lloyd Wright rang in the modern era with a leap forward in materials, avant-garde design, and use of space. And Graceland is still teaching us that you just can't have too much shag carpeting or too many fuzzy pillows.

If you have too many girlfriends at one time it's nothin' but trouble. They get upset, you get upset, your wife gets upset, and it's just a big ol' mess.

It's important to believe in a higher power. Even if the Colonel insists that you keep makin' awful bad movies.

It don't matter if people want the fat you or the skinny you. The important thing is that they want you.

Look at it this way—the fatter you are, the more sequins you get to wear.

You've got to be firm with children. Especially when they're your wife.

What's done is done. No use worryin' about it.
Heck . . . they wanted me for the lead in *West
Side Story,* but the Colonel wouldn't let me do
it. So what if that coulda catapulted my acting
career? So what if that one morsel of creativity
might've made it worthwhile for me to get up in
the mornin'? So what if I still wake up screamin',
"I could-a met a freakin' girl named Maria—"

But I *didn't!!* I mean . . . so what?

It's not often that a man is very good at two things. But if you're lucky enough to have someone like that in your employ, you hang on to him. That was the case with Larry Geller, my spiritual advisor and hairdresser.

If your wife tells ya she's takin' Lisa Marie to the store with her to buy more white lipstick and hairspray, and that she'll be right back, *do not* believe her.

You know that sayin', "Keep a stiff upper lip"?
Yeah, that's way overrated.

Your hair can be downright "pompadourable," if you comb it just right.

Hey, solid gold toilet seats are gonna be a little chilly in the winter, man, but no pain, no gain.

In life it's very important to keep the proper perspective. Because unless you know just how far away an object is, it's very difficult to shoot it.

If a woman goes to the trouble of throwin' her underwear at you, it's only right to reciprocate by sweatin' on a scarf and givin' her that.

Getting good grades in high school is very important. Now, I may be a rock star, but I was always very strict about that with my wife.

As a young adult ya gotta work hard to have a good relationship with your momma and daddy. I guess I just tried harder than most kids did. Well, that and I bought 'em houses and cars and stuff.

Bundle up in the wintertime or you'll catch a cold. So button that shirt all the way up past your navel.

Always stretch before strenuous gyration. Talk about pullin' a groin, man.

It's good to be the King.

When purchasing a mink coat for your five-year-old, make sure you buy it a couple-a sizes too big.

When you triumphantly throw your arms skyward during the finale of "Burning Love," that jumpsuit's gonna ride up in crevices you didn't even know you had. Just be ready for it is all I'm sayin'.

Not only does the key to a city not open anything, but just try to keep that daggone thing on your key chain! Them things are huuuuuge, man!

The secret to getting spotted in fast-food restaurants is to spend a lot of time in fast-food restaurants.

Invest in yourself. I paid four dollars to Sun
Records to make my first recording back in
1953. Let's see . . . that's like a 50 million
percent return. I don't know much about math,
but they tell me that's good.

If it looks like an Elvis, talks like an Elvis, and walks like an Elvis, it's probably an Elvis, but it ain't necessarily me.

Nothin' boosts a man's confidence like wearin' a cape.

One good way to tell the difference between dusk and dawn is to spill somethin', then wait to see if the day maid or the night maid cleans it up.

Listen to your loved one's concerns. One time Priscilla said, "Elvis, you look blue." And I said, "Well, I guess I am a little sad." And she said, "No. I mean your skin is actually blue." Dang if she wasn't right too!

Don't displace your anger. I remember when Colonel Parker screwed me out of my deal to star with Barbara Streisand in *A Star Is Born* by asking for too much money, then booked me for six months of grueling tour gigs instead. I was so mad, I went right out and bought some stuff I didn't need, then blew my doghouse to bits with a sawed-off shotgun.

Wait . . . that's a bad example.

No matter how famous you get, don't let people treat you special.

OK, I am *totally* kidding, man!

When your name is three stories high and towering behind you in neon lights, you no longer need a name tag.

It's important to stay grounded. I remember
when Priscilla wanted to go out and party with
the stars. I'd have to remind her, "Priscilla,
you're only fourteen years old. I grounded you
for comin' in late last night, and darn it, you're
gonna stay grounded!"

Always leave 'em wanting more.

Save everything. I once blew my nose on a napkin and it went for like $5,000.

120 LIFE LESSONS FROM ELVIS

Be it on the ceiling or the floor, nothin' says class like shag.

In one movie I'd be a singing race-car driver, but then in my next film, I'd be a singing motorcycle racer. And then I'd be a singing speedboat racer! Diversity is the key to making it in Hollywood.

Marriage is give and take. For example . . .
Priscilla once asked me to *give* her some lovin'
and I *took* a nap.

Life is like Beale Street. You start out at one end bright-eyed and bushy-tailed, and wind up on the other end—worn out, broke, a little tipsy, and wishin' you could do it all over again.

Lay off-a them *light* blue suede shoes after
Labor Day.

Old habits are hard to break. When I first went into the service, I was so used to bein' managed by Colonel Parker, that every time I saw an officer I'd give 'em 25 percent of my salary.

Remember, it's always skinny to fat . . . skinny to fat. It just ain't right to hang a collection of my commemorative plates any other way.

Now, I don't know nothin' about the origin of the universe. But I do know that the origin of Priscilla's hairstyle in the early '70s can be explained by the "Big *Bangs* Theory."

Be sure to vote. Just look at the last election and you see what can happen if you don't! You wouldn't believe how many people are still complainin' about the "older me" not bein' on that postage stamp.

Enjoy the little things in life. For example, compared to all your other achievements, having your postage stamp be the most popular one in U.S. history may not seem like much, but . . . wait . . . those of you without commemorative postage stamps might think that is a pretty big deal, huh? So . . .uh . . . hey look, stop and smell the roses is all I'm sayin'!

Time waits for no one. But it goes by faster watchin' one-a-them Elvis clocks where my legs wiggle back and forth with each second. Now that's just daggone clever, man.

Blue suede is the new black velvet.

The secret to acting is to play yourself in every movie. Course, then it's more like "being" than "acting."

Advice and medication should be taken the same way—very carefully—with the option to throw it up if it starts to make you sick.

Marriage is hard work. Don't let anybody tell you otherwise. That's why I took a lot of vacations with my girlfriends.

You know you're in denial when you surround yourself with people who agree with everything you say. Ain't that right, Red?

Red says yes.

No shirt, no shoes, no Graceland.

If your wife wakes you up before you've gotten your fifteen hours of sleep, shoves a pen in your hand, and tells you you're signin' a contract for a movie called "Divorce Settlement," *do not* believe her.

Ya never know where inspiration's gonna come from. I was on a date with this stuttering chick and she said, "Elvis, I want you, I need you, I-hi-hi-hi I love you." And *bam!* I had a hit.

Remember: "More self-help" ain't the same thing as "helpin' yourself to more."

When decorating a room, it's the subtleties that make the difference. Even though people might not notice them right off, their subconscious will remember these tiny details later. A throw pillow and knickknack here, lime green shag carpeting on the ceiling there. You'd be surprised.

If you can stand face-to-face with a woman in the rain without her getting wet, you know your hair is just right.

Just cuz you're wearin' a cape doesn't mean you can fly. Man, I learned *that* the hard way.

As an artist, you have to have an appreciation for all the different mediums. That's why I've familiarized myself with the various schools of painting: Impressionism, Realism, Abstractionism, and Black Velvetism.

Don't forget where you came from. When I went back home to Tupelo in 1956, people were screamin', swoonin', and faintin'. Now, that's cuz they had just put up their first traffic light. But they were happy to see me too.

Let's see . . . there's the Black Elvis, the Little Kid Elvis, the Asian Elvis, the Woman Elvis, the Fat Elvis, the Skinny Elvis, the Dwarf Elvis, the Ice-Skating Elvis, the Santa Elvis, the Hawaiian Elvis, the Chimpanzee Elvis, the Skydiving Elvis, and Elvis-the-Clown.

And that's just what's goin' on in *my* head! Don't even get me started on those impersonators, man.

Sometimes you have to sacrifice for your art. I mean, I never did, but that's what I've heard.

A person's environment greatly influences their appearance. Don't fight it! Being from Mississippi, I developed a smooth, cool, Southern style and a huge appreciation for great clothes. Priscilla, on the other hand, was born in Brooklyn and grew up in Germany, which accounts for her great appreciation for huge hair and smooth, cool European style.

A broken heart is like a broken guitar string. It makes an ugly twangy noise when you're in the middle of a chord and then just dangles there. Now maybe that don't make no sense, but neither does love, man. Neither does love.

Demand the original whenever you can. They broke the mold after they made me, but that hasn't stopped people from tryin' to glue it back together ever since.

A marriage without love is like a jungle room
without a waterfall.

Be modest and understated.

Naw, I'm just kiddin', man!

Seriously though, there is such a thing as too much success.

Naw, I'm just kiddin' again, man!

What comes around goes around. I started out in Tupelo with a lot-a big dreams in a little shotgun shack and ended up in Memphis in a big shack with a lot-a shotguns.

It's never too late to gyrate.

I've thought a lot about it, and I just don't think life is like a box of chocolates. I mean, what does an empty box have to do with life?

Sometimes, your encore doesn't begin 'til you *leave* the building.

I have left the building.

ABOUT ANTHONY RUBINO JR.

When Elvis was pushing thirty-two, he had recently presented Priscilla with an engagement ring, given more than $100,000 to charity, and on a whim purchased seventeen horses for his family and friends. That same week, Elvis's latest film, *Spinout,* had just premiered and Anthony Rubino was born. They're both still receiving mixed reviews.

Anthony has also written *Life Lessons from Melrose Place, Life Lessons from the Bradys,* and *1001 Ways to Procrastinate.* When Anthony's not attempting to make sense of life through popular culture, he spends his time in New York City being an artist, creative director, and the undisputed Heavyweight Champion of the World.

What? OK, not so much that last thing. He's also a nationally syndicated cartoonist and has written for publications including *Mad* and *National Lampoon.*

Visit him at www.rubinocreative.com.